How to Read
Food Product Labels

Mason Crest
450 Parkway Drive, Suite D
Broomall, PA 19008
www.masoncrest.com

Printed and bound in the United States of America.

First printing
9 8 7 6 5 4 3 2 1

Series ISBN: 978-1-4222-2874-6
Hardcover ISBN: 978-1-4222-2880-7
ebook ISBN: 978-1-4222-8942-6
Paperback ISBN: 978-1-4222-2993-4

The Library of Congress has cataloged the
        hardcopy format(s) as follows:

                Library of Congress Cataloging-in-Publication Data

Etingoff, Kim.
  How to read food product labels / Kim Etingoff.
     pages cm. – (Understanding nutrition : a gateway to physical & mental health)
  Audience: Grade 4 to 6.
  Includes bibliographical references and index.
   ISBN 978-1-4222-2880-7 (hardcover) – ISBN 978-1-4222-2874-6 (series) – ISBN 978-1-4222-2993-4 (paperback) – ISBN 978-1-4222-8942-6 (ebook)
  1. Food–Labeling–Juvenile literature. 2. Food–Composition–Juvenile literature. 3. Nutrition–Juvenile literature. I. Title.
   TX551.E88 2014
   664'.09–dc23

                        2013009803

Produced by Vestal Creative Services.
www.vestalcreative.com

UNDERSTANDING NUTRITION:
A GATEWAY TO PHYSICAL AND MENTAL HEALTH

How to Read
Food Product Labels

KIM ETINGOFF

Mason Crest

CONTENTS

Introduction 6
1. Why Should You Pay Attention to Food Labels? 9
2. Understanding Serving Size 17
3. Understanding Calories 25
4. Understanding What Your Body Needs:
Adding Up the Percentages 33
Find Out More 46
Index 47
About the Author & Consultant and Picture Credits 48

INTRODUCTION
by Dr. Joshua Borus

There are many decisions to make about food. Almost everyone wants to "eat healthy"—but what does that really mean? What is the "right" amount of food and what is a "normal" portion size? Do I need sports drinks if I'm an athlete—or is water okay? Are all "organic" foods healthy? Getting reliable information about nutrition can be confusing. All sorts of restaurants and food makers spend billions of dollars trying to get you to buy their products, often by implying that a food is "good for you" or "healthy." Food packaging has unbiased, standardized nutrition labels, but if you don't know what to look for, they can be hard to understand. Magazine articles and the Internet seem to always have information about the latest fad diets or new "superfoods" but little information you can trust. Finally, everyone's parents, friends, and family have their own views on what is healthy. How are you supposed to make good decisions with all this information when you don't know how to interpret it?

The goal of this series is to arm you with information to help separate what is healthy from not healthy. The books in the series will help you think about things like proper portion size and how eating well can help you stay healthy, improve your mood, and manage your weight. These books will also help you take action. They will let you know some of the changes you can make to keep healthy and how to compare eating options.

Keep in mind a few broad rules:

- First, healthy eating is a lifelong process. Learning to try new foods, preparing foods in healthy ways, and focusing on the big picture are essential parts of that process. Almost no one can keep on a very restrictive diet for a long time or entirely cut out certain groups of foods, so it's best to figure out how to eat healthy in a way that's realistic for you by making a number of small changes.

- Second, a lot of healthy eating hasn't really changed much over the years and isn't that complicated once you know what to look for. The core of a healthy diet is still eating reasonable portions at regular meals. This should be mostly fruits and vegetables, reasonable amounts of proteins, and lots of whole grains, with few fried foods or extra fats. "Junk food" and sweets also have their place—they taste good and have a role in celebrations and other happy events—but they aren't meant to be a cornerstone of your diet!

- Third, avoid drinks with calories in them, beverages like sodas, iced tea, and most juices. Try to make your liquid intake all water and you'll be better off.

- Fourth, eating shouldn't be done mindlessly. Often people will munch while they watch TV or play games because it's something to do or because they're bored rather then because they are hungry. This can lead to lots of extra food intake, which usually isn't healthy. If you are eating, pay attention, so that you are enjoying what you eat and aware of your intake.

- Finally, eating is just one part of the equation. Exercise every day is the other part. Ideally, do an activity that makes you sweat and gets your heart beating fast for an hour a day—but even making small decisions like taking stairs instead of elevators or walking home from school instead of driving make a difference.

After you read this book, don't stop. Find out more about healthy eating. Choosemyplate.gov is a great Internet resource from the U.S. government that can be trusted to give good information; www.hsph.harvard.edu/nutritionsource is a webpage from the Harvard School of Public Health where scientists sort through all the data about food and nutrition and distill it into easy-to-understand messages. Your doctor or nurse can also help you learn more about making good decisions. You might also want to meet with a nutritionist to get more information about healthy living.

Food plays an important role in social events, informs our cultural heritage and traditions, and is an important part of our daily lives. It's not just how we fuel our bodies; it's also but how we nourish our spirit. Learn how to make good eating decisions and build healthy eating habits—and you'll have increased long-term health, both physically and psychologically.

So get started now!

1

Why Should You Pay Attention to Food Labels?

Do you ever wonder what's in your food? What exactly is an apple made out of? Why does that hamburger taste so good?

Or maybe you're wondering about what kinds of food are healthy. What should you eat? What should you stay away from?

A good place to start answering these questions is by looking at food labels. You can find food labels on just about every food that has a package.

Almost all foods have labels on the back or side of the package, can, or box. Look for the nutrition facts on the next food you eat.

Food labels list all sorts of things. They list ingredients. They list how many vitamins and minerals a food has. They list how much sugar and fat a food has. You can find out a lot just by looking at the label.

Where Do I Find Food Labels?

Most packaged foods have labels. They are usually on the side or the back of the package.

Canned foods have labels. Frozen dinners have labels. Juice has labels. Cereal has labels. Pretty much anything you find in the grocery store has a label!

A few foods don't have food labels. For example, **produce** usually doesn't. Fresh fruits and vegetables are sold piece by piece. You put them in a bag yourself.

Sometimes things sold in big packs of ten or more don't have food labels either. If you buy a twelve-pack of juice boxes, each one doesn't have a food label. But the big package they all came in does.

The Info

A food label has a lot of information on it. There are a lot of numbers. It can be confusing to look at if you don't know what the words and numbers mean.

Food labels list different nutrients you find in food. Nutrients are substances that people need to live. Our bodies can't make them. We have to eat food to get them. You've probably heard of vitamin C and calcium. Those are just two nutrients. There are lots more.

When you look at a food label, you can see what nutrients are in that food. And you can see how much of each nutrient is in there. Nutrients are sometimes measured in grams. A paper clip weighs a little more than a gram.

Sometimes food only has tiny amounts of nutrients. Then the nutrients are measured in milligrams. A milligram is tiny. It's much smaller than a gram. A small snowflake weighs about a milligram.

What Is Produce?

Produce are foods that have been grown, like fruits and vegetables.

Guide to Food Label Words

Here's an explanation of what all of those words on a food label mean.

Calories: A measure of how much energy a food has.

Calories from fat: How much of the food's energy comes from fat.

Serving size: The amount of the food that someone is likely to eat at one time. All the rest of the information is based on how much of each nutrient is found in that amount.

Servings per package: How many servings are in the entire container.

Total fat: The amount that's in the food of a substance that keeps our skin and other organs healthy.

Saturated fat: The kind of fat found in meat and dairy products. (It's best to limit how much saturated fat you eat.)

Unsaturated fat: This kind of fat is found in vegetables and nuts. (This is a healthier kind of fat.)

Trans fat: This is a kind of fat made in factories. Trans fat is not good for you.

Cholesterol: Another kind of fat that comes from meat and dairy products. We need a little but not a lot.

Sodium: Another name for salt.

Carbohydrates: These are nutrients that supply the energy our bodies need.

Sugar: A kind of carbohydrate that tastes sweet.

Dietary fiber: A kind of carbohydrate that people don't digest but that keeps our digestive systems healthy.

Protein: A nutrient that keeps our muscles and blood healthy.

Vitamin A: A nutrient that keeps skin, teeth, and eyes healthy.

Vitamin C: A nutrient that helps our body repair itself when it is hurt.

Calcium: A mineral our body needs for strong bones.

Iron: A mineral that keeps our blood healthy.

Daily Values

Food labels wouldn't be very useful if all they had were lists of nutrients and how much the food has of each one. There would be something missing.

You have to know how much of each nutrient we need. Do we need a lot of calcium or just a little? Is 200 calories a lot or a little? How much vitamin C do we need every day?

That's why food labels also list something called a daily value. If you look on the right side of the label, you'll see a bunch of percentages. Those are called daily values.

A food label might say, for example, that your food has 30 milligrams of cholesterol. It also says that is 20 percent of your daily value. What does that mean?

You need 100 percent of every nutrient, every day. So if your food has 20 percent of what you need in a day, that means you need 80 percent more. In this case, doing some math, that means you need 120 more milligrams.

The daily values are the most helpful numbers. You don't really know how much of a nutrient you need. So the grams and milligrams aren't really helpful. But you can look at the daily value. Then you'll always know.

If something has 100 percent daily value, that's all you need! If it has 50 percent, that's half of what you need. It's a good way to practice your math too!

Ingredients

The other big part of a food label is the ingredient list. The ingredient list is just what it sounds like. It's a list of everything that's in the food you're about to eat.

Sometimes the ingredient list is simple. On milk, the ingredient list is just "milk." When you read it, you know that nothing else was added in.

On a package of cookies, the ingredient lists might be really long. There are a lot of things in store-bought cookies. You can get an idea of what you're eating when you read the ingredient list.

The biggest ingredients are listed first. The ingredients that are smaller are listed at the bottom. So, for a loaf of bread, flour would come first. Then water, oil, sugar, yeast, and salt. Bread is mostly flour. So flour comes first. There's only a little bit of the other ingredients.

A Cookie's Ingredients

Here's a list of everything found in a store-bought cookie. You might not even be able to pronounce a lot of the ingredients!

Enriched bleached wheat flour (flour, niacin, reduced iron, thiamine mononitrate, riboflavin, folic acid), powdered sugar (sugar, cornstarch), sugar, margarine (palm oil, water, soybean oil, salt, contains two percent or less of: mono- and diglycerides, calcium disodium EDT [preservative], artificial flavor, annatto color, vitamin A palmitate), water, eggs, rice flour, contains two percent or less of: nonfat milk, whey protein concentrate, lactose, leavening (sodium acid pyrophosphate, baking soda, monocalcium phosphate), food starch-modified, vegetable oil (palm kernel and/or palm oil and/or partially hydrogenated cottonseed and soybean oils), cornstarch, cellulose gum, carrageenan, soy lecithin (emulsifier), confectioner's glaze, gum arabic, artificial flavor, titanium dioxide, gum tragacanth, red 3 & 40, red 40 lake, yellow 5 & 6, yellow 5 & 6 lakes, blue 1 & 2, blue 1 & 2 lakes, polysorbate 60, sodium propionate (preservative).

Reading Food Labels for Health

Food labels aren't meant to be confusing! They're a good tool. They can tell you if a food is healthy or not.

Healthy foods have a lot of vitamins and minerals. So the daily values for vitamins and minerals will be high. Look for big numbers for dietary fiber, protein, vitamin A, vitamin C, calcium, and iron. When you see those big numbers on a food label, it means that food is a healthy choice.

Unhealthy foods have a lot of stuff that isn't good for you. The daily values for the less healthy stuff will be high. High numbers in fat, cholesterol, sodium, and sugar aren't so good. Try to eat less of those foods.

Food labels are also good if you have **allergies**. If you're allergic to eggs, you can look at the ingredient list. If you see "eggs" in the list, you know you shouldn't eat that food.

Once you know how to read food labels, you'll be able to pick up a food and know if it's healthy or not, just by reading the label!

What Are Allergies?

When your body overreacts when you eat something, that's called an **allergy**. You might get an itchy mouth. Or break out in a rash. Serious allergies can make you really sick. Lots of people have food allergies. Peanuts and other nuts are common allergies. Some people are allergic to shellfish (like shrimp). And eggs. And soy. You have to stay away from foods if you're allergic to them. Otherwise, you could have an unpleasant reaction or even get really sick!

Nutrition Facts

Serving Size: 1 Can

Amount Per Serving

Calories 150

	% Daily Value*
Total Fat 0g	0%
Sodium 55mg	2%
Total Carb. 40g	13%
Sugars 40g	
Protein 0g	

ant Daily Values a
,000 Calories
TED

2

Understanding Serving Size

When you read a food label, you'll find serving size at the top of the label. In fact, it's the very first thing at the top. Serving size is the key to the rest of the food label. Once you can figure it out, you can read the rest of the label.

What Is It?

Serving size is a certain amount of food. It could be an ounce of cheese. Or a cup of orange juice. Or 10 crackers.

Nutrition Facts

Serving Size   1 Cup (53g/1.9 oz.)
Servings Per Container   About 8

Amount Per Serving

Calories 190	Calories from Fat 25

% Daily Value*

Total Fat 3g	**5**%
Saturated Fat 0g	**0**%
Trans Fat 0g	
Cholesterol 0mg	**0**%
Sodium 100mg	**4**%
Potassium 300mg	**9**%
Total Carbohydrate 37g	**12**%

Paying attention to serving sizes and how many servings are in the package is an important part of making healthy food choices. Serving sizes can help you make better decisions about portion sizes and balancing your diet.

The rest of the information on the food label is based on the serving size. The food label lists how many calories are in one serving. And how much sodium. And carbohydrates. And vitamin A. And everything else that's on the label!

Food companies come up with serving size. Sometimes they're based on how much you actually eat at one time. But not always. Sometimes you eat more than a serving size. Sometimes you eat less.

Using Serving Size

Understanding serving size uses a little bit of math. Let's take a look at milk to understand a little better what serving size is.

A gallon of 1% milk says the serving size is one cup. Does that mean there's only one cup in the whole container? No, there's a gallon. There are actually 16 cups in a gallon. So we're only looking at a little bit of milk. Not the whole container.

Are you going to drink one cup? Probably. One cup is about a glass full. You probably drink about a cup of milk at a time.

The food label on 1% milk says there are 105 calories in a serving. The milk also has 2.38 grams of fat in a serving. That's 4 percent of your daily value. Also, there are 313.6 milligrams of calcium. That's 31 percent of your daily value.

The milk has 105 calories, 2.38 grams of fat, and 313.6 milligrams of calcium per serving. And you're drinking one serving. Easy! You know that glass of milk you're drinking has exactly those amounts of nutrients.

But what if you wanted two glasses of milk? How many nutrients would you be getting then? Now your serving size is "2." You're drinking 2 cups of milk (which is about the same as two glasses).

So you'll have to multiply by two. You'll be drinking twice as many calories:

105 calories x 2= 210 calories
You'll need to multiply everything else by 2 as well:

2.38 grams of fat x 2= 4.76 grams of fat
4% x 2= 8% of your daily value of fat

Serving sizes are fixed numbers for each kind of food you eat, but portion sizes are up to you to decide. You can choose to eat one serving, or you can choose to eat more than one serving.

How to Read Food Product Labels

313.6 milligrams of calcium x 2= 627.2 milligrams of calcium

31% x 2= 62% of your daily value of calcium

So now you've learned some things about the milk. You know that drinking two glasses of 1% milk gives you a lot of calcium. It also is low in fat, which is good. One percent milk is a healthy thing to drink!

You can find out the same thing with any food label. Follow these steps:

1. Find the serving size.
2. Figure out how many serving sizes you're eating.
3. Multiply the nutrients by how many servings you're eating.

Then you have to use what you know about nutrition. Are there too many calories? Are there enough vitamins? What about fat? Keep doing **research**. Pretty soon you'll have a good idea about what makes a food healthy or not.

Serving Size and Portion

Serving size is not the same as a portion. A portion is how much you choose to eat. You might eat half a granola bar, one granola bar, or two granola bars. Your portion would be half, one, or two.

Serving size isn't up to you. The food label tells you the serving size. For granola bars, the serving size is probably one bar. If you ate half a granola bar, you would be eating half a serving. One granola bar would be one serving. Two granola bars would be two servings.

What Is Research?

Research is what you do when you want to find out an answer to a question. Research is looking for answers. You could do research by going to the library and reading books. You could do research on the Internet. You can also do research by asking people who might know more than you do about something.

Checking the number of calories in the package and the number of calories per serving is one of the best ways to keep track of how much you're eating.

That's pretty easy. It can get more complicated, though.

Imagine you're eating some crackers. You just can't stop. You eat 30 crackers. Your portion is 30.

Now you look at the box to find the serving size. It's only 10 crackers! You ate 3 times that many (10 x 3 = 30). This means you ate 3 servings.

It's not always bad to eat more than one serving. If you eat three servings of carrots, that's great! The right portion depends on what kind of food it is that you're eating. Serving size doesn't tell you what you *should* eat. Only you can decide that.

Bigger and Bigger

People are eating more and more these days. Portions are getting huge! In the past, people ate smaller meals. Now we've gotten used to being really full at every meal. In the 1970s, a normal bagel was three inches across. It had 140 calories. Today, bagels are 6 inches across. They have 350 calories. We think that's normal! But up until a few years ago, people would have thought that bagel was too big. Such big portions add up. A lot of people (including kids) weigh too much. That's partly because we eat so much.

Nutrition Facts

Serving Size 1 Apple (125 g)

Amount Per Serving

Calories 65 | Calories from Fat 2

% Daily Value*

Total Fat 0g	0%
Saturated Fat 0g	0%
Trans Fat	
Cholesterol 0mg	0%
Sodium 1mg	0%
Total Carbohydrate 17g	6%
Dietary Fiber 3g	12%
Sugars 13g	
Protein 0g	

Vitamin A	1%	Vitamin C	10%
Calcium	1%	Iron	1%

*Percent Daily Values are based on a 2,000 calorie diet. Your daily values may be higher or lower depending on your calorie needs.

3

Understanding Calories

People talk about calories a lot. From the way they talk, you might think calories are bad for you. But that's not true! Calories are really important. Without calories, you wouldn't be able to live. Calories measure the part of food that keeps us going.

Energy

Food gives us energy. We need food because we need energy. If people didn't eat, they wouldn't be able to live. They wouldn't have enough energy to move around. Or think. Or breathe. Everything we do uses energy.

Calories are sort of like the fuel we put in our cars. In the same way we have to fill up our cars with gas, we need to keep our bodies feuled with energy from food. Healthier food makes for better feul, so making healthy food choices is important to keep you at your best.

Think about a car. You have to put gasoline in a car to make it go. Gasoline is the fuel that gives it energy. The car burns the fuel and turns it into energy so that it can move. Instead of gas, people need food. Food is like our fuel. Our bodies turn the food into energy.

Calories are a way to measure that energy. A food with a lot of calories will give us a lot of energy. A food with just a few calories won't give us much energy.

Calories are a way to measure something. You measure height with inches. You measure weight with pounds. You measure liquid with cups or ounces. And you measure energy with calories. You can't see energy, so it might be a little more confusing to think about. But scientists have figured out how to measure the energy that's found in foods.

Food labels list calories so we know how much energy we're getting. Calories are right near the top of a food label.

Good and Bad

When people want to lose weight, they try to cut calories. They burn them up as fast as they can by exercising.

Calories aren't bad for you. Everyone needs them to live. People need calories to go to school. They need them to play sports. They even need them to watch TV and play computer games.

The choices people make about calories are what make them a problem. If you eat too many calories, you'll gain weight. And gaining too much weight is unhealthy. Then you might have to stop eating so many calories. Or start exercising more.

And some calories are better than others. Not all calories are the same. The best calories come in foods that also have lots of vitamins and minerals. That way, the calories we're eating are worth it. We're staying healthy because the calories come with vitamin D, iron, potassium, and other nutrients.

Calories that don't come with any vitamins and minerals aren't as good. Usually the not-so-good calories are found in foods that are really sugary or really salty. There might be a lot of calories along with a lot of unhealthy things. These are called empty calories.

Calories that come from sugar don't give us energy that lasts very long. Think about what happens when you eat a candy bar. You get a lot of energy right away. You might

Breakfast

LOW-FAT YOGURT AND FRUIT — 250 CALORIES
CHOCOLATE DOUGHNUT — 270 CALORIES
WHOLE-GRAIN CEREAL WITH SKIM MILK — 140 CALORIES
BAGEL AND CREAM CHEESE — 450 CALORIES
* BISCUIT WITH SAUSAGE, EGG AND CHEESE — 570 CALORIES

Lunch

TUNA SALAD SANDWICH ON WHOLE WHEAT BREAD — 215 CALORIES
GRILLED CHICKEN WRAP — 250 CALORIES
GRILLED SALMON SALAD — 300 CALORIES
PIZZA (2 SLICES) — 540 CALORIES
* BURGER, FRIES, SODA (SMALL MEAL) — 839 CALORIES

Dinner

SALAD WITH TUNA — 300 CALORIES
GRILLED CHICKEN BREAST, BROWN RICE, AND VEGETABLES — 450 CALORIES
SPAGHETTI WITH TOMATO SAUCE — 450 CALORIES
7OZ SIRLOIN STEAK, STEAMED POTATOES, AND VEGETABLES — 550 CALORIES
* PIZZA (2 SLICES) — 540 CALORIES

This chart shows some examples of foods you might eat at breakfast, lunch, and dinner. Keeping track of calories is the best way to make sure you're not eating more than the number you need each day.

want to run around. But that only lasts for a little while. Then you start to feel tired. You crash.

Calories from healthier foods don't do that. They give you energy for a long time. They're much better for you.

Counting Calories

Some people count every calorie they eat. Sometimes, that's okay. But most of the time, you don't need to do that. You should focus on eating healthy instead. Eat nutritious foods. And don't eat too much. If you follow those rules, you won't need to spend time figuring out how many calories you eat. Food should be fun! Not a chore.

The Right Amount

We need about 2,000 calories a day to be healthy. Some people might need 1,600 calories. Others need 2,500 calories.

How many calories you need depends on a few things. Girls usually need fewer than boys. People with lots of muscles need more. Taller or naturally heavier people need more calories too.

Everything you do needs calories. Just sitting and breathing uses some. Not many, though. Walking and running use more. Playing sports use a lot. The more you move, the more calories you burn.

Calories have a lot to do with how much you weigh. You can gain weight by eating too many calories. You can lose weight by not eating enough calories. Or by using up more calories than you eat.

Along with making healthy food choices, getting plenty of exercise is the best way to stay healthy and lose weight. Any exercise will burn more calories than sitting around, so get up and get active!

The average person needs 2,000 calories a day. In other words, the average body uses 2,000 calories a day walking around, pumping blood, and breathing. You also eat about 2,000 calories every day. Since the number of calories you lose and eat are the same, you stay the same weight.

Then you start to play soccer after school. Now you burn 300 calories every day. You need to eat 300 more calories to stay the same weight. But you don't really eat any more. You're using more calories than you're eating. So you start to lose weight.

Suppose you realize you're losing weight. So you eat start eating cheeseburgers and ice cream for every meal. Now you eat 3,000 calories every day. You're eating way more calories than you're using. You'll start to gain weight now!

If you're a healthy weight, you probably don't have to worry about calories too much. You should just make sure you eat healthy. Eat lots of fruits and vegetables. Eat whole grains. Don't eat a lot of food with sugar and salt.

If you need to lose weight, it's good to think about calories a little. You know that you're eating more calories than you're using. You have two choices. You can eat less. That means that maybe you should skip the ice cream after dinner. Or eat a healthier lunch. It doesn't mean you should stop eating!

Or you could start using more calories than you're eating. You could exercise more. Join a sports team. Walk to and from school. Ask a friend to start running with you. You have lots of choices!

How Many Calories?

Every food and drink except water has calories. Here's a list of how many calories some foods have:

- 1 banana = 105 calories
- 1 plain bagel = 360 calories
- 8 oz. low fat chocolate milk = 158 calories
- 1 cup whole wheat spaghetti = 176 calories
- 1 cup raw carrots = 50 calories
- 6 fast-food chicken nuggets = 360 calories
- 1 cup vanilla ice cream = 273 calories

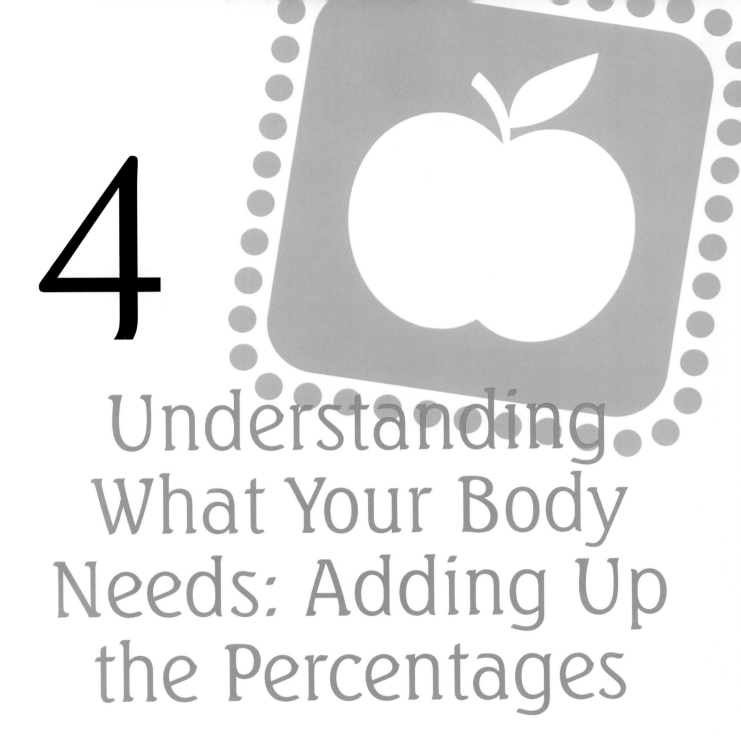

4

Understanding What Your Body Needs: Adding Up the Percentages

N ow you know more about all those words and numbers on the food label. Let's take a look at what they mean to you.

Guide to Nutrients

Lots of people know that they should eat vitamins and minerals. But they don't know why. Here are some of the reasons we should (and shouldn't) eat each nutrient on a food label.

Dietary Fat

Unsaturated Fat	Saturated Fat	Trans Fat
Food Examples	**Food Examples**	**Food Examples**
Almonds Vegetables Fish Olives Olive Oil	Beef Butter Pizza Ice Cream Lard	Cookies Donuts Cakes Fries Hydrogenated Oil
Benefits	**Benefits**	**Benefits**
Works in conjunction with saturated fats to prevent heart attacks and strokes Raises good cholesterol levels	Works in conjunction with unsaturated fats to prevent heart attacks and strokes	None

There are three kinds of fat in the foods we eat. While we need some fat in our diet, trans fat is very unhealthy and should be avoided whenever possible. You can find out how much of each kind of fat is in the food you eat by checking food labels.

FAT

Fat keeps our skin and organs healthy. Fat also gives us energy. And it carries around other nutrients, like vitamins A and D. We need to eat some fat!

Too much of the wrong kind of fat isn't good, though. Most people only need a little every day. Too much fat can make you gain weight. It can make your heart unhealthy.

The best kinds of fat are unsaturated. The kinds of fat to stay away from are saturated and trans fat. Good fats (unsaturated) are in avocados, nuts, and olive oil. Bad fats (saturated and trans) are in meat, dairy, and margarine.

CHOLESTEROL

Cholesterol helps form hormones (things that carry messages in our body). It builds up cell walls. It helps make vitamin D.

Again, we want to eat a little cholesterol. Your body needs a little bit of it every day. But a lot of cholesterol causes heart disease. So try not to eat very much cholesterol every day if you want to stay healthy. Cholesterol is in hamburgers, bacon, and other meat. It's also in dairy products.

SODIUM

Sodium is another word for salt. People need a little sodium every day. Sodium helps our nerves and muscles work right. It also balances how much water is in our bodies. Our body is mostly water. Sodium keeps the water in the right places.

Too much sodium, though, can cause heart and blood problems. Some people with heart disease have to keep track of how much sodium they eat.

Sodium is in just about everything. Chips, crackers, cheese, and even sports drinks—they all have a lot of sodium. Pay attention to how much sodium is in the foods you eat. Don't eat too much of it!

CARBOHYDRATES

Carbohydrates are how we get most of our energy. There are lots of kinds of carbohydrates. Two of them are listed on food labels: fiber and sugar. Fiber keeps your digestive system healthy. It's good for you to eat a lot of fiber.

Nutrition Facts

Serving Size 1 cup (228g)
Servings Per Container about 2

Amount Per Serving

Calories 250   Calories from Fat 110

	% Daily Value*
Total Fat 12g	**18%**
Saturated Fat 3g	**15%**
Trans Fat 3g	
Cholesterol 30mg	**10%**
Sodium 470mg	**20%**
Total Carbohydrate 31g	**10%**
Dietary Fiber 0g	**0%**
Sugars 5g	
Proteins 5g	
Vitamin A	4%
Vitamin C	2%
Calcium	20%
Iron	4%

* Percent Daily Values are based on a 2,000 calorie diet. Your Daily Values may be higher or lower depending on your calorie needs:

	Calories:	2,000	2,500
Total Fat	Less than	65g	80g
Saturated Fat	Less than	20g	25g
Cholesterol	Less than	300mg	300mg
Sodium	Less than	2,400mg	2,400mg
Total Carbohydrate		300g	375g
Dietary Fiber		25g	30g

1. **Serving Size**

2. **Amount of Calories**

3. **Limit These Nutrients**

4. **Get Enough of These Nutrients**

5. **Percent (%) Daily Value**

6. **Footnote With Daily Values (DVs)**

Food labels show how much of your daily percentages you're getting from the food you eat. You can check for fat, sugars, protein, vitamins, and more on all food labels.

Try to limit how much sugar carbohydrates you eat, though. That energy gets used up very quickly. And too much sugar can cause all sorts of health problems, like weight gain and **diabetes**.

Fiber is in whole grains (like whole-wheat bread). It's in fruits and vegetables. It's in beans.

Sugar is in most things that come in packages, not just sweet things like cake and candy.

PROTEIN

Protein helps you grow strong. It makes your muscles healthy. It also is a good source of energy. And it helps your body repair itself when you get cut, break a bone, or get hurt some other way.

Meat has protein in it. So do lentils, beans, dairy products, and nuts. It's hard to get too much protein. Eat foods with lots of it.

VITAMIN A

We need vitamin A to see. We also need it for healthy teeth and skin. Not eating enough vitamin A can lead to eye problems, and even blindness. It's hard to get too much of it.

Some vitamin A comes from animal foods, like fish and milk. Vitamin A also comes from plants, especially orange-colored ones, like carrots and sweet potatoes.

What Is Diabetes?

Diabetes is a kind of sickness that some people get when they weigh too much. Even kids can get diabetes. Diabetes is a sickness in which your body can't use sugar the way it's supposed to. There are two kinds of diabetes. One is called Type 1 diabetes. It is usually passed on from parents to children. Type 1 diabetes doesn't really have much to do with a person's weight. Someone who is a healthy weight can get Type 1 diabetes. People with Type 1 get it when they are kids and have to give themselves shots of something called insulin. The shots help their bodies use sugar normally.

The other kind of diabetes is Type 2 diabetes. Being overweight or obese can cause it. People with Type 2 diabetes don't usually have to get shots, but they do have to watch what they eat. They will have to exercise and lose weight. They are more likely to get sick later on than people without diabetes. For example, they could get heart disease or kidney failure. It's much better to avoid getting Type 2 diabetes in the first place!

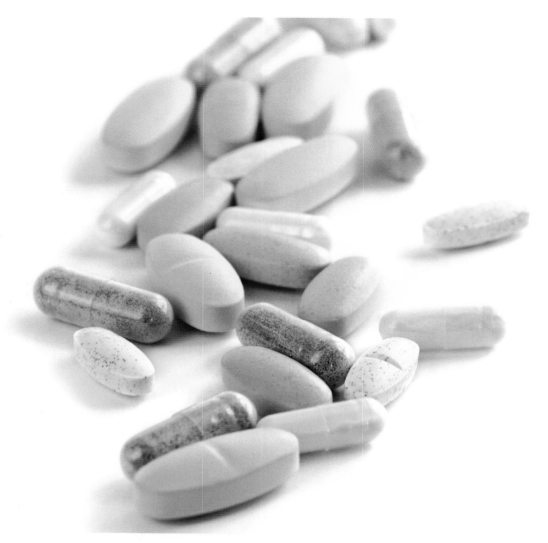

You should try to eat a balanced diet and meet all of your daily percentages, but sometimes eating enough of each nutrient is difficult. Many people choose to take vitamin pills to get enough of the vitamins and minerals that we all need to stay healthy.

VITAMIN C

Vitamin C protects our cells from things like pollution and sunlight. This vitamin also helps our body heal wounds and fight sicknesses.

It is also hard to eat too much vitamin C. It is water soluble, which means we get rid of any extra vitamin C in our bodies whenever we urinate.

Fruits and vegetables have a lot of vitamin C. Citrus fruits like oranges and grapefruits have a lot. Sometimes cereal and other foods have vitamin C added to it.

CALCIUM

Calcium makes strong bones and teeth. Muscles and nerves also use calcium. Without calcium, your bones would get weak and break more easily.

You might already know that milk and other dairy has a lot of calcium. So do dark green vegetables, like kale and spinach. And some foods have calcium added in to them so that people get an extra boost.

IRON

Iron keeps up our energy. Iron in the blood brings oxygen to every part of the body. That keeps our bodies feeling energetic. Iron also keeps our skin and hair healthy.

Not eating enough iron is pretty common. Anemia is caused by not having enough iron. Anemia makes people tired. Eat more shellfish, beans, meat and vegetables to avoid being anemic. Sometimes iron is added into food too.

Vitamins and Minerals

People usually say "vitamins and minerals" in the same sentence. They're two different things though. Plants and animals make vitamins. Minerals come from dirt and water. Plants and animals can't make minerals. But plants do suck them up from the dirt and water. And animals eat them. Then we eat the plants and animals. We get the minerals too. Vitamins and minerals have something in common. People's bodies can't make enough of them. So we have to get both vitamins and minerals from food.

Processed foods are often made with lots of sugar, fat, and salt. Fruits and vegetables are much healthier and don't have any of ingredients that make processed foods so unhealthy.

High and Low

So what does all this mean? We need a little of every nutrient on a food label. But we don't always need a lot of each one.

A food is healthy because it has a lot of good nutrients. You can use a food label to figure out if a food is healthy. Just look for big numbers of good nutrients.

Healthy foods have some unsaturated fat. They have a lot of dietary fiber. They have a lot of protein. They have a lot of vitamins A and C. They have a lot of calcium and iron.

Healthy foods are also low in the nutrients we only need a little of. Healthy foods have little or no saturated fat. They have only a little cholesterol. And only a little sodium and sugar.

Unhealthy foods are the opposite. They have a lot of cholesterol, sodium, and sugar. They only have a little bit of fiber, protein, vitamins, and minerals.

These are the keys to knowing if a food is healthy or not. Remember what you need a lot of, and what you need a little of. Then you won't need to add up numbers or do much math.

Reading the Ingredient List

The other part of the food label is the ingredient list. Reading the ingredient list is another way to help you figure out if a food is healthy or not.

The healthiest foods usually have the shortest ingredient lists. Processed foods usually have long lists. Processed foods are foods made in factories. Chips are processed foods. So is candy. And doughnuts.

Processed food usually has a lot of salt, sugar, and fat. They don't have good vitamins and minerals. You should only eat processed foods sometimes, not for every meal and snack.

Processed foods also have lots of ingredients that are hard to pronounce. A good tip is to eat more foods that have ingredients you can pronounce!

Stay away from foods that have certain ingredients at the top of the list. Unhealthy foods list "sugar," "high fructose corn syrup," "sucrose," and "salt" in the top few ingredients.

INGREDIENTS: CULTURED GRADE A REDUCED FAT MILK, APPLES, HIGH FRUCTOSE CORN SYRUP, CINNAMON, NUTMEG, NATURAL FLAVORS, AND PECTIN. CONTAINS ACTIVE YOGURT AND L. ACIDOPHILUS CULTURES.

Reading the ingredients list on the foods you eat is very important. You can learn a lot by reading the names of the ingredients in your food. Try to stay away from foods that are made with high fructose corn syrup, a type of sugar. Many sugary snacks and drinks are made with this unhealthy syrup, so be sure to check the nutrition facts to see what your next snack is made of and see if you can make a healthier choice.

Add Up Your Own Percentages

Remember daily value? Those are the percents on a food label. They show you how much of each nutrient you're getting. They compare that to how much you need in a day.

Keep a food journal. In your journal, write down everything you eat for a day. This is where food labels come in.

Use each food's label to write down how many calories you eat and the daily values of each nutrient you eat.

If you eat a bowl of cereal, a banana, and some juice for breakfast, write it all down. Write down the food label info for the cereal. Remember to use serving size to figure out how much you're eating. If you eat two servings, you have to double the calories and nutrients on the food label.

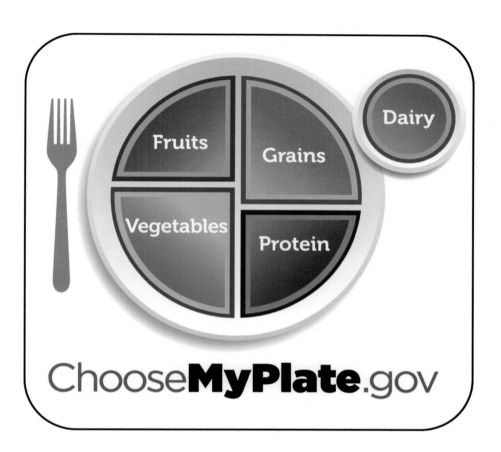

Governments around the world tell their people about healthy eating in different ways. In the United States, MyPlate shows Americans how much of each kind of food they should each in each meal. By using food labels and guides to eating a balanced diet, you can make healthier food choices.

Write down the milk. And the juice. Use the food labels on the packages. For the banana, look up its nutrition info online. There are lots of websites where you can find food label info, even for foods that don't have food labels!

Do that for the rest of the foods you eat. Then, at the end of the day, do some math! Add up all the calories. Add up the daily values for fats, protein, and the rest.

How did you do? You should have eaten somewhere around 2,000 calories. And 100 percent of your daily value for each nutrient.

Fresh fruit and vegetables don't have food labels, of course, but they are the healthiest foods you can choose. If you want to keep track of the calories you're eating in fresh fruit, you can check online for calorie counters that tell you how many calories are in the apple you ate for lunch.

You probably didn't eat perfectly. That's okay! Lots of people don't eat as healthy as they should. But now you can figure out what you need to do to eat better. You know what you need more of. And what you need less of.

Talk to a doctor if you're worried. Doctors can give you good advice about how to eat healthy. Each person is different. You might need more or less calories. You might need to eat more of a certain nutrient. Your doctor will know and can help you out.

You can do a lot on your own, though. Food labels give us lots of clues about food. If you make a habit of reading them, you'll start to learn what's good for you and what isn't. You can make good choices—choices that will help you stay healthy and strong.

No Food Labels

The best foods to eat don't even have food labels! Fresh fruits and vegetables are great things to eat. Fruits and vegetables are high in all the good things. They have fiber. They have vitamins and minerals. And they're low in the not-so-good things. Fruits and vegetables have some natural sugars. They don't have much cholesterol or bad fat. They don't have much sodium. And they don't have labels.

Find Out More

ONLINE

Calorie Count
www.caloriecount.about.com

KidsHealth: Figuring Out Food Labels
www.kidshealth.org/kid/stay_healthy/food/labels.html

KidsHealth: Keeping Portions Under Control
www.kidshealth.org/parent/nutrition_center/healthy_eating/portions.html

PBS Kids Go! Food Smarts: Understanding Food Labels
www.pbskids.org/itsmylife/body/foodsmarts/article4.html

IN BOOKS

Burstein, John. *Looking at Labels: The Inside Story*. New York: Crabtree Publishing, 2008.

McCarthy, Rose. *Food Labels: Using Nutrition Information to Create a Healthy Diet*. New York: Rosen Publishing, 2008.

Pollan, Michael. *The Omnivore's Dilemma: The Secrets Behind What You Eat, Young Readers Edition*. New York: Dial Books, 2009.

Index

allergies 15

calcium 11–14, 19, 21, 39, 41
calories 5, 7, 12–13, 19, 21–23, 25–31, 42–45
carbohydrates 12, 19, 35, 37
cholesterol 12–13, 15, 35, 41, 45
corn syrup 41–42

daily values 13–15, 42–43

energy 12, 25–27, 29, 35, 37, 39
exercise 7, 30–31, 37

fat 7, 11–12, 14–15, 19, 21, 31, 34–36, 40–41, 43, 45
fiber 12, 14, 35, 37, 41, 45

ingredients 11, 13–14, 40–42
iron 12, 14, 27, 39, 41

math 13, 19 ,41, 43, 47
minerals 11, 12, 14, 27, 33, 38–39, 41, 45

nutrient(s) 11–13, 19, 21, 27, 33, 35, 41–42

packages 9–13, 18, 22, 37, 43
percents 5, 13–14, 19, 21, 33, 36, 38, 42–43
portion 6-7, 18, 20–21, 23, 46
potassium 27
processed 40–41
protein 7, 12, 14, 36–37, 41, 43

serving size 5, 12, 17-21, 23, 42
snacks 41–42
sodium 12, 14–15, 19, 35, 41, 45
sports 6, 27, 29, 31, 35
sugar 11–15, 27, 31, 35–37, 40–42, 45

vitamins 11–14, 19, 21, 27, 33, 35–39, 41, 45

weight 6, 27, 29–31, 35, 37

About the Author & Consultant

Kim Etingoff lives in Boston, Massachusetts, spending part of her time working on farms. Kim has written a number of books for young people on topics including health, history, nutrition, and business.

Dr. Borus graduated from the Harvard Medical School and the Harvard School of Public Health. He completed a residency in Pediatrics and then served as Chief Resident at Floating Hospital for Children at Tufts Medical Center before completing a fellowship in Adolescent Medicine at Boston Children's Hospital. He is currently an attending physician in the Division of Adolescent and Young Adult Medicine at Boston Children's Hospital and an Instructor of Pediatrics at Harvard Medical School.

Picture Credits